EXPLORING THE CANADIAN ARCTIC

# The Northern Environment

by Annalise Bekkering

Weigl

Published by Weigl Educational Publishers Limited
6325 10 Street SE
Calgary, Alberta
T2H 2Z9

www.weigl.com

Library and Archives Canada Cataloguing in Publication

Bekkering, Annalise
           The northern environment / Annalise Bekkering.
(Exploring the Canadian Arctic)
Includes index.
ISBN 978-1-55388-961-8 (bound).
ISBN 978-1-55388-965-6 (pbk.)

1. Natural history--Canada, Northern--Juvenile literature.  2. Canada,
Northern--Environmental conditions--Juvenile literature.  I. Title.
II. Series: Exploring the Canadian Arctic (Calgary, Alta.)

QH106.2.A7B45 2009              j508.719              C2009-903468-9

Printed in the United States of America
1 2 3 4 5 6 7 8 9 0  13 12 11 10 09

Project Coordinator: Heather Kissock
Design: Terry Paulhus

All of the Internet URLs given in the book were valid at the time of publication. However, due to the dynamic nature of the Internet,
some addresses may have changed, or sites may have ceased to exist since publication. While the author and publisher regret any
inconvenience this may cause readers, no responsibility for any such changes can be accepted by either the author or the publisher.

Every reasonable effort has been made to trace ownership and to obtain permission to reprint copyright material. The publishers
would be pleased to have any errors or omissions brought to their attention so that they may be corrected in subsequent printings.

Weigl acknowledges Getty Images as its primary image supplier for this title.
Mary Hopson: page 24 left; Kris Light: page 24 middle; Joy Viola: page 24 right; Bill Steele: page 25 left;
Gary Mussgnug: page 25 right.

We gratefully acknowledge the financial support of the Government of Canada through the Book Publishing Industry Development
Program (BPIDP) for our publishing activities.

# Contents

# Beyond 60 Degrees

C anada's Arctic region is a vast area that covers more than 40 percent of the country's total land. Nunavut, Northwest Territories, Yukon, and the northern tip of Quebec make up this northern area.

Any land in Canada above 60 degrees latitude is considered the North. This imaginary line became the border of the Arctic region when Saskatchewan and Alberta were declared provinces in 1905.

With almost total darkness in the winter and near total sunlight in the summer, Canada's Arctic region is known as the Land of the Midnight Sun. Here, much of the land is permanently frozen, and trees cannot grow. Shrubs, mosses, and lichens are the only plants that can survive the cold climate. Temperatures may reach more than 20 degrees Celsius in the summer, but the season is very short and wet.

The unique environment in Canada's Arctic is threatened by many different factors. Although it is far from heavily populated areas, the Arctic environment is still affected by influences from thousands of kilometres away. This fragile **ecosystem** is threatened by human activities, such as pollution, industry, and climate change. If such activities are allowed to continue, environmental damage in the Arctic could have a devastating impact on the rest of the world.

The rugged mountains, sweeping glaciers, and polar sea ice of Auyuittuq National Park showcase the special features of the Arctic environment.

# A History of Change

O ver millions of years, the climate of the North has experienced many changes. Its temperatures were both colder and warmer in the past than they are today.

Scientists studying in the area have found evidence that the Arctic had a much warmer climate about 45 millions years ago. They have located ancient **fossilized** forests on Axel Heiberg Island that share similar features to trees that grow today in much warmer climates.

As well as plants, scientists have found several fossils of animals that live in much warmer climates. These animals include rabbits, beavers, horses, and even lemurs. These finds have led scientists to conclude that the Arctic may have had a tropical climate that was lush with forests and other vegetation.

As well as its fossilized forests, Axel Heiberg Island is home to more than 1,100 glaciers.

About two million years ago, the North turned cold and snowy with the start of the Pleistocene epoch, or the last Ice Age. **Glaciers** moved over the land and eventually spread southward, covering most of North America.

The weight of all this glacial ice had a tremendous impact on the land, pushing it down in places. These "glacial thrusts" are believed to have created the lowland coastal areas of the Arctic Archipelago, a group of islands lying north of Canada's mainland.

The Ice Age ended about 10,000 years ago. Most glaciers receded until only the places nearest the North Pole remained covered in ice. Although freezing temperatures are still common in the North, average temperatures continue to rise. Some scientists predict winter temperatures in the region will rise by 5 to 10 degrees Celsius in the next century.

■ The Kaskawulsh Glacier, in Yukon's Kluane National Park, has existed for more than 10,000 years. Like many glaciers, it is gradually receding. Its meltwaters are flowing into the Pacific Ocean and the Yukon River.

■ Fossils can provide scientists with much information about the history of a region.

# NORTHERN LANDFORMS

The North consists of many landforms, such as pingos, glacial cirques, and tors, that are not found in more temperate climates. Pingos are cone-shaped hills that have a core of clear ice. Some pingos stretch as high as 90 metres. Glacial cirques are bowl-shaped depressions that are partially surrounded by steep cliffs. They are formed by glacial **erosion**. The highest cliff in a glacial cirque is often called a "headwall." Tors are tower-like features that stand above a smooth surface. They are formed by a long period of **weathering**.

# Mapping the North

ARCTIC OCEAN

Canada's North is often regarded as an ice-covered barren terrain. In fact, the North has a variety of geographical features, ranging from mountains to significant bodies of water and the world's largest archipelago. The Arctic Archipelago consists of more than 20 separate islands and occupies about 1.3 million square kilometres.

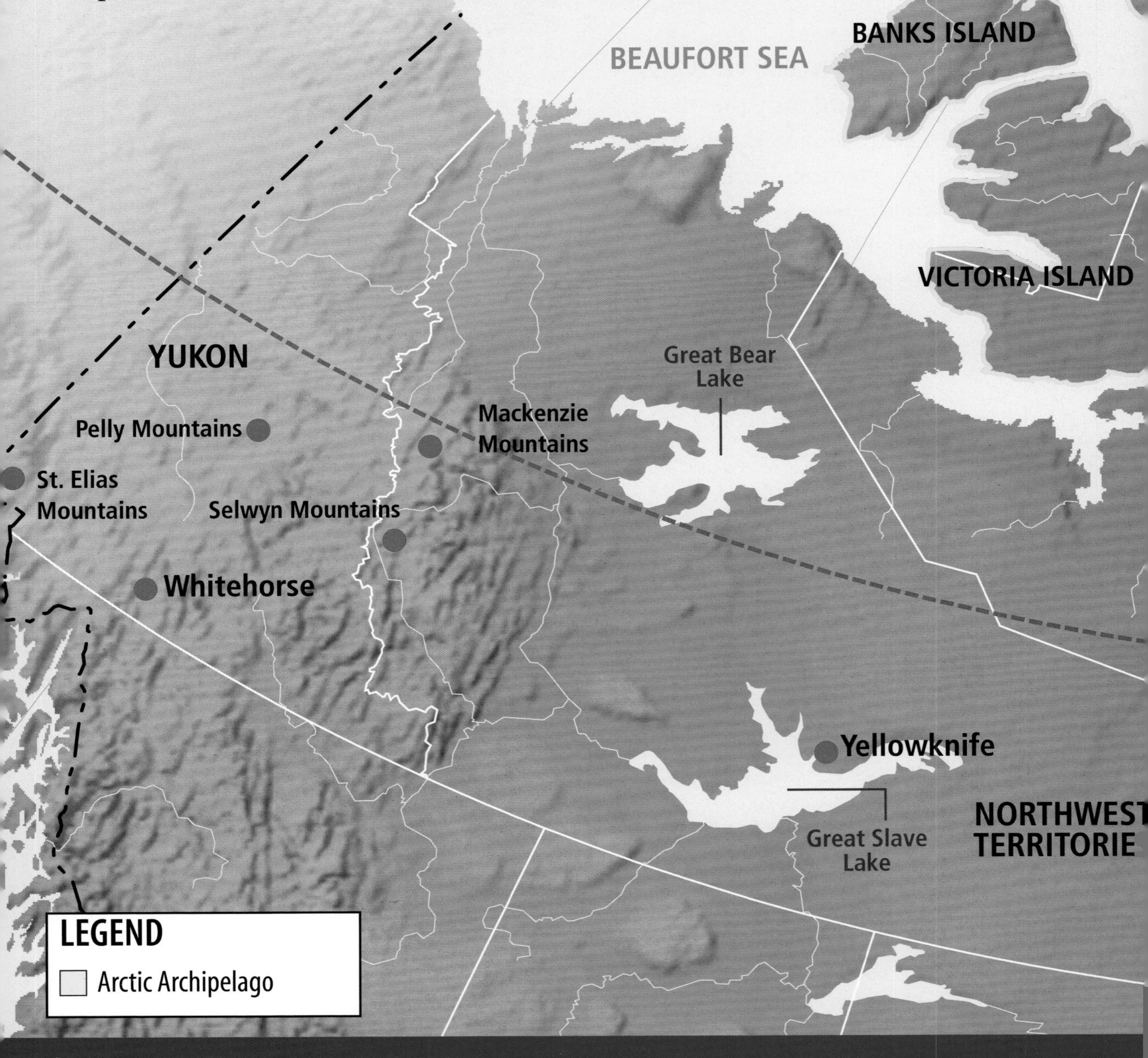

McClure Strait

BANKS ISLAND

BEAUFORT SEA

VICTORIA ISLAND

YUKON

Great Bear Lake

Pelly Mountains

Mackenzie Mountains

St. Elias Mountains

Selwyn Mountains

Whitehorse

Yellowknife

NORTHWEST TERRITORIE

Great Slave Lake

## LEGEND

☐ Arctic Archipelago

ELLESMERE ISLAND

AXEL HEIBERG ISLAND

GREENLAND

DEVON ISLAND

Viscount Melville Sound

Lancaster Sound

PRINCE OF WALES ISLAND

BAFFIN ISLAND

KING WILLIAM ISLAND

Arctic Circle

Iqaluit

NUNAVUT

HUDSON BAY

QUEBEC

60 Degrees Latitude

# The Fragile Arctic

Canada's northern environment is very fragile. It is a delicate balance of climate, landforms, plants, animals, and bodies of water. All of these depend on each other for sustainability. Small changes in any of these factors can lead to significant changes in the overall environment of the North.

The past century has seen major changes take place in the North. The main cause of these changes has been human development, whether it originates in the North itself or comes from other parts of the world.

As technology has developed over the years, it has led to two major global problems—global warming and pollution. Global warming occurs when **greenhouse gases** trap energy from the Sun in Earth's atmosphere, which creates heat. This raises the temperature on the planet.

■ Polar bears live mainly on sea ice. Due to global warming, the sea ice is melting and the bears are losing their habitat.

Over the past 100 years, Earth's temperature has risen about 1 degree Celsius. In the Arctic, however, summer temperatures have risen by about 1.2 degrees Celsius per decade since the 1980s. This slight, but constant, temperature increase has had a negative impact on the plants and animals that base their survival on a colder climate.

Pollution from humanmade chemicals and substances also affects the global atmosphere. Pollutants are absorbed into water vapour and blown by strong winds, before falling to Earth in the form of **acid rain**, harming plant and animal life in the region.

Pollution comes from other parts of the world as well as Canada's North itself. As industry, in the form of mining, grows in the North, still more pollution is being created. Industrial development is also taking over the land, causing animals and plants to lose their natural habitat. With loss of habitat, some of the world's most unique life forms may also be lost.

■ The heavy machinery used in mining Arctic resources contributes to the pollution in the area.

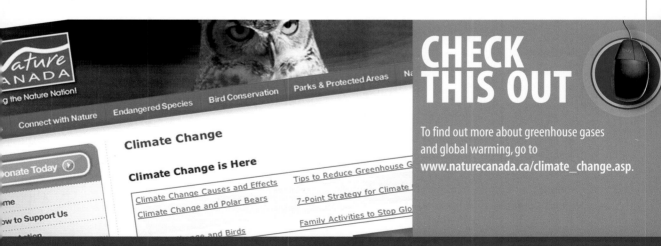

# A Changing Climate

Arctic temperatures are rising two times faster than the rest of the world. This is partly due to the burning of fossil fuels, such as natural gas and oil, throughout the world. Burning fossil fuels is producing greenhouse gases.

Rising temperatures are affecting the permafrost that covers most of the Arctic's land. The permafrost is, in effect, melting. As the permafrost thaws from global warming, the vegetation growing in it decays at a faster rate than normal. This increases the amount of carbon dioxide in the atmosphere and speeds up global warming even more.

The effects of global warming extend to Arctic waters as well. Global warming is causing sea ice to melt more than it has in the past. As this ice melts, it becomes salt water. Salt water sinks, creating ocean currents. These currents pull warmer water from the south toward the Arctic. Warmer water flowing into the Arctic increases the temperature of the air and water. Warmer air and water temperatures cause more sea ice to melt.

As the sea ice loses its thickness and melts away, it is causing water levels to rise. Over time, rising water levels may lead to extreme flooding, not only in the Arctic, but in other parts of the world as well. Melting of Arctic ice could cause sea levels throughout the world to rise by 0.9 metres.

## First-hand Account

### Lucassie Arragutainaq

Weather has become unpredictable for people living in the North. Climate change has affected the seasons in the Arctic and has impacted the way of life for many people living there.

"Even if we try to predict what it is going to be like tomorrow...the environmental indication isn't what the Elders said it would be. Sometimes, it is still true but sometimes it isn't. In the past, when they said, 'it's going to be like this tomorrow,' it was. But our weather and environment are changing so our knowledge isn't true all the time now.

We're being told [in Hudson Strait] that maybe if we put January, February, or March one month behind, our knowledge of weather would be more accurate, because the weather in those months isn't the same anymore."

Global warming has a profound impact on the food chain in the North. Animals use the sea ice for a variety of purposes. Polar bears travel on the ice to hunt ringed seals. Ringed seals hide underneath the ice to avoid polar bears and other predators. The loss of sea ice is contributing to a loss of habitat for these animals.

Land animals are also experiencing changes to their way of life. Cotton grass, an important food source for migrating caribou, now blooms earlier than usual on the tundra because of the warmer winters. Caribou arrive too late to feed on the cotton grass bloom. They must search for other food sources.

## Ice Coverage

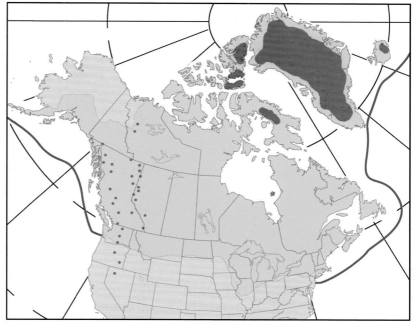

## LEGEND

- Principal areas formerly covered by glacial ice
- Principal areas now covered by glacial ice
- Maximum limit of sea ice

## PERMAFROST

Permafrost is permanently frozen ground. It can extend 1,000 metres into the ground. As global temperatures rise, permafrost thaws, having a devastating impact on humans and the landscape. For example, thawing permafrost on a mountain can lead to landslides and increase erosion of coastlines. Poorly constructed buildings on permafrost can warm up the ground, thaw the permafrost, and destroy the building.

# Land Development

Over the past 100 or so years, the North has become known throughout the world for its abundant natural resources. Beginning with the Gold Rush of the 1800s, people have been coming to northern Canada to locate and extract the many minerals found there. These minerals include gold, oil, natural gas, diamonds, and zinc. The processes involved in mining, such as digging and drilling, are greatly affecting the land and disrupting the life forms that rely on it.

The transportation of these products is leading to changes in the land. Oil and natural gas are transferred to refineries using pipelines. Other minerals are transported by tractor-trailers. The construction of pipelines and roads degrades the land, destroying fragile ecosystems that have been in place for thousands of years.

As more and more people come to the North to work and live, infrastructures must be adjusted to accommodate them. This means that more land is developed for human habitation. Houses, stores, and office buildings are being constructed at the expense of the natural environment.

## First-hand Account

### Don Russell

Don Russell from Canadian Wildlife Services has commented on caribou survival and pipeline expansion in the Yukon Territory.

"Whatever happens in the winter affects the calf survival, affects the pregnancy the next year and virtually every aspect of productivity from age of first reproduction to calf survival."

■ As more people move to the North, the need for housing is growing and changing. The pre-built houses of the 1970s are being replaced by larger and grander homes.

Human impact on the land is upsetting the natural balance of the food chain. Plants called lichens grow throughout the Arctic tundra. These small plants are a mainstay in the diet of many animals. Caribou, for one, feed on lichen. Destruction of the landscape along migration routes leads to decreased lichen. Once lichens are destroyed, a forest can take between 80 to 150 years to produce enough lichens for migrating caribou.

■ As cities grow in population, they expand in size. Construction projects are taking unused land and developing it for housing and other structures, all at the expense of the natural environment.

Fragile ecosystems are being impacted by human development. About 15 percent of all the world's species of birds spend their breeding season in the Arctic. The birds' breeding grounds are becoming threatened because of habitat loss. The loss of breeding areas for these birds could affect other ecosystems throughout the world.

# ECO-TOURISM

Environmentally friendly travel is called eco-tourism. Eco-tourist expeditions strive to have little or no impact on the environment. There are many opportunities for eco-tourism in Canada's Arctic. Eco-tourists can observe Arctic animals, such as caribou and polar bears, in their natural habitat and see parts of the world that very few people have seen before. Although the goal of eco-tourism is to protect the environment, it can still be a threat to the plants and animals in the Arctic. People may unknowingly disrupt migrating birds and animal habitats. As eco-tourism becomes popular, many more people may come to visit the Arctic, increasing the environmental impact. Canada, Finland, and Sweden have developed programs to educate tourism companies and tourists about respecting the Arctic while travelling.

# A Polluted North

**H**umanmade pollutants have been a worldwide problem for years. Even though much of the North remains a wilderness area, it has not been untouched by this global problem. In fact, as human development increases in the area, the North is beginning to become part of the global problem.

Emissions from vehicles and industry contribute to global warming, and they put dangerous gases into the air. While some of these gases arrive in the North via wind currents, others are created by industrial development in the North itself. Construction equipment gives off dangerous gases in its exhaust. Digging into the ground for mining purposes releases toxic gases that are hidden in the soil. Oil spills from tanker ships make oil a dangerous pollutant in Arctic waters. Ocean currents can send this pollutant into waters that are farther away, causing problems for the bodies of water in other parts of the world.

Even nature itself now contributes to the problem. Migratory birds are capable of carrying pollution to the North from other areas of the world. They deposit pollutants, such as PCBs, dioxins, and mercury, in their droppings. These toxic chemicals can stay in the environment for years. They are eaten and digested by animals, which are then eaten by people. These pollutants can have dangerous effects on animal and human health.

Canadian Arctic Resources Committee
A voice for citizens on the Canadian North for more than 30 years

Home   About CARC   Issues   CARCHIVE   Support CARC

2030 NORTH
2030 North - A National Planning Conference

Welcome to the CARC Website!
citizens' organization dedicated to the long-
and social well being of northern
in sustainable

## CHECK THIS OUT

To read more about pollution in the Arctic, go to www.carc.org/pubs/v18no3/1.htm.

Pollution from petrochemical plants thousands of kilometres away spew toxins into the air. Winds carry these toxins to other parts of the world, including the Arctic.

# Aboriginal Perspectives

Respect for the environment is important to many Aboriginal groups. This is especially true in the Arctic, where Aboriginal Peoples still depend greatly on the land for food, water, and shelter. Most Aboriginal Canadians believe that people should only take what they need from Earth. This belief promotes the idea of protecting Earth for future generations.

In order to protect their environment, Canada's northern Aboriginal Peoples have begun incorporating sustainable technology into their communities. This technology allows them to create comfortable living spaces that have little impact on the environment.

Rankin Inlet, Nunavut, has become a leader in this area. In 2000, the community began using a wind turbine to generate electricity for houses and buildings. Wind power is an environmentally friendly alternative to burning fossil fuels, which is a more common way to obtain power. Rankin Inlet's wind turbine saves the community from using 40,000 litres of diesel fuel every year.

In addition, Rankin Inlet receives many hours of sunshine during spring and summer. This sunshine is used to generate solar energy. The local high school has installed solar panels to heat the school. These panels harness the Sun's rays and convert them into electricity. This saves the community 2,600 litres of fuel every year. Other communities have followed suit. The people of Fort Smith, Northwest Territories, have installed solar panels on the community centre. These panels save the community 6,370 litres of fuel per year.

Wind turbines are being erected all over the world as a way to reduce the use of fossil fuels in energy creation.

Solar panels are a clean and environmentally sound way to collect solar energy.

Rankin Inlet is located on the west coast of Hudson Bay. It has a population of about 2,400.

# CHECK THIS OUT

Read more about Rankin Inlet's solar panels at
**http://nature.ca/sila/dvtr/slrwll_e.cfm.**

# Environment Then and Now

Canada's Arctic environment has experienced many changes over time. What was once a region with lush vegetation and exotic animals became overrun with snow and ice. Now, a new cycle is occurring, with warmer temperatures returning to the area. However, this change is contributing to a degradation of the land due to human pollution and development.

■ Permanent ice cover in the Arctic is decreasing at a rate of nine percent each decade. If this trend continues, summers in the Arctic could be ice-free by the end of the century.

| THEN | NOW |
|---|---|
| **TEMPERATURE** | |
| In parts of the Arctic, average summer temperatures were about 5 degrees Celsius. | In 2007, temperatures in the Arctic rose to 22 degrees Celsius in the summer. Ice that is normally 2 metres thick was only 1 metre thick that summer. |
| **WINTER ICE COVERAGE** | |
| From 1979 to 2000, winter ice coverage in the Arctic was spread out over about 15.9 million square kilometres. | In the winter of 2009, Arctic ice covered 15.1 million square kilometres. |
| **SEASONAL ICE** | |
| In the 1980s and 1990s, **seasonal ice** accounted for only 40 to 50 percent of the Arctic's total ice coverage. | In 2009, seasonal ice accounted for 70 percent of the Arctic's total ice coverage. This suggests that glacial ice is disappearing from the Arctic at a rapid rate, mainly due to global warming. |
| **CONDITION OF PERMAFROST** | |
| Permafrost held the land together and kept it firm. | Permafrost is thawing. This is causing coastal shorelines to erode. Animals that rely on the Arctic environment are losing their habitat. Buildings that were constructed on the firm permafrost are now in danger of sinking into what are now wetland areas. |
| **LAND DEVELOPMENT** | |
| The first Arctic oil well in Canada was dug in 1920. Between 1950 and 1960, more than 350 wells were dug in the Arctic. | Advanced technology, mapping, and drilling have contributed to more than 1,900 oil and gas wells in the Arctic. |

# Pipeline Expansion

# AT ISSUE

Canada's Arctic is rich with resources, including natural gas. The world market for natural gas has made drilling in the Arctic a profitable business. In order to get the gas to other parts of the continent, companies have proposed a pipeline be built from the Beaufort Sea to the United States. The pipeline would run more than 1,200 kilometres through the forests along the Mackenzie River.

Many people are in favour of the pipeline. Its construction would bring more people to the Arctic and would increase drilling for gas. The pipeline would also benefit the economy of Canada's Arctic and create jobs.

Environmentalists, however, are concerned about the proposed pipeline. It could interfere with caribou migration, further threatening the caribou population. It may also affect permafrost. The pipeline may be warmer than the ground and melt the permafrost. Melted permafrost would cause the land to heave and shift, changing the landscape and threatening animal habitats.

## Should Pipelines Be Built in the Arctic?

A debate occurs when people research opposing viewpoints on an issue and argue them following a special format and rules. Debating is a useful skill that helps people express their opinions on specific subjects.

1. Decide how you feel about the issue described.

2. Ask a friend to argue the opposing viewpoint.

3. Use the information in this book and other sources to prepare a two-minute statement about your viewpoint.

4. Present your argument, and listen while a friend gives his or her argument. Make notes, and prepare a response.

5. Present your rebuttal and a final statement. Let your friend do the same. Did your friend's arguments change how you feel about the issue?

# Plants at Risk

Whether by land development, global warming, or pollution, habitat destruction usually impacts an ecosystem's smallest residents first before gradually working its way up the food chain. The Committee on the Status of Endangered Wildlife in Canada (COSEWIC) has been monitoring the changes occurring in Canada's North in relation to the plants and animals that live there.

## ARCTIC SPRING BEAUTY

The Arctic spring beauty can be found at elevations up to 2,000 metres. This flowering herb is a perennial, which means it lives for at least two years. It blooms in June and July each year. Its flowers range from white to pink.

## ARCTIC WORMWOOD

Also known as purple wormwood, this small shrub-like plant grows on gravelly tundra slopes. It can be found at elevations ranging from 200 to 1,300 metres. Arctic wormwood is a perennial that blooms in June and July. It can grow to about 16 centimetres in height, but its average height is 9 centimetres.

## FELT-LEAF WILLOW

Felt-leaf willow is a perennial shrub. Its presence in the North has been compromised by the construction of roads and pipelines. However, steps are being taken to replant it in other areas. This willow is normally found in rocky soils along riverbanks and sandbars and can grow up to 10 metres tall.

As a result of their research, they have identified more than 20 plants that could be at risk of disappearing from their northern habitat. Some of these plants have already been listed as endangered species, while others are on the committee's watch list.

## SPOTTED LADY'S SLIPPER

The spotted lady's slipper is found in the Yukon and Northwest Territories. Growing up to 30 centimetres in height, each stem features a single flower, which is white with pink to red markings. It flowers in June and July in the forests, tundra, and meadows of the North.

## WALPOLE'S POPPY

Walpole's poppy is found in the Yukon, as well as the U.S. state of Alaska. It grows in exposed upland areas of the tundra at elevations up to 900 metres. Walpole's poppy is a perennial herb that flowers from late May to August. Its petals can be yellow or white.

## YUKON WHITLOW GRASS

Yukon Whitlow grass is known as the rarest plant in Canada. A member of the mustard family, Yukon Whitlow grass is found only in the Kluane region of the Yukon. It does not, however, grow in the protected area of Kluane National Park, which means it is vulnerable to destruction by construction projects.

# A Thaw in the Ground

**A**bout 50 percent of Canada's landmass rests on permafrost, much of it in Canada's North. As a result of global warming, the permafrost is starting to thaw in several regions. This is having an effect on the natural environment, as well as land development in the North. In the northernmost regions, this thawing is resulting in less permafrost and more fertile land. In the southernmost parts of the region, there is a strong possibility that permafrost will disappear entirely. This can have a range of consequences for the North.

In terms of the natural environment, thawing permafrost will cause the landscape to change. As plants will be able to extend their roots farther into the ground, different types of plants will creep up into the northern habitat. What was once tundra could eventually become boreal forest. This will have a negative impact on animals and plants that have adapted to live in a colder climate. The thaw may also create instability in the land itself as it is no longer frozen, making the area more susceptible to landslides.

Unstable land will have a negative effect for the land development that has already take place in the North. Soft land will cause structures, such as houses, office buildings, and pipelines, to sink into the ground. Landslides have the potential to harm entire communities.

This map indicates where permafrost thaw would have the greatest impact on the land. Generally, the areas that are of most concern are those that contain large amounts of ice under the permafrost. These are the regions that could become the most unstable if the permafrost were to thaw too much or too quickly. Areas in the southern regions would not be as affected by thawing as their permafrost coverage is not as thick, and there is more fertile soil in the region to help stabilize the land.

PHYSICAL RESPONSE TO WARMING

Low

Moderate

High

Massive Ice

Glacier

# Quiz

What have you learned about the environment in the Canadian Arctic?
Take this quiz to find out.

**1** | When did the last Ice Age end?

**2** | Name three northern landforms.

**3** | What is the Arctic Archipelago?

**4** | Name three major threats to Canada's northern environment.

**5** | What is permafrost?

# 6 | What is the goal of eco-tourism?

## 7 | How do birds pollute the North?

## 8 | Which northern community has become a leader in sustainable development?

## 9 | How many oil and gas wells are in the Arctic?

## 10 | How much of Canada's landmass rests on permafrost?

Answers:

1. About 10,000 years ago
2. Pingos, tors, and glacial cirques
3. A group of more than 20 separate islands that cover about 1.3 square kilometres of Canada's North
4. Global warming, land development, pollution
5. A layer of permanently frozen ground
6. To have little or no impact on the environment
7. By carrying pollutants, such as PCBs, dioxins, and mercury, from other locations in their droppings
8. Rankin Inlet
9. More than 1,900
10. About 50 percent

# Thawing Permafrost

**P**ermafrost is found under much of Canada's boreal forest and Arctic tundra. It is even found on the floor of the ocean off the Arctic coast. This frozen ground defines the ecosystems of the North. On the tundra, permafrost prevents trees from anchoring their roots deep into the ground. It also stops water from absorbing into the soil. Try this activity to help you understand how permafrost works.

**What you will need**
  two shallow baking pans
  soil
  tap water
  fork
  tablespoon
  toothpicks
  modelling clay
  freezer

1. Fill both pans with moist soil to a depth of about 5 centimetres.

2. Place one of the soil-filled pans into the freezer overnight. Set the other soil-filled pan on a countertop. What do you think will happen to the soil in the freezer?

3. The next day, remove the pan from the freezer. Set it next to the unfrozen soil, and compare.

4. Use the fork to determine which soil is harder.

5. Pour a spoonful of water on the frozen soil. Watch what happens. Do the same to the unfrozen soil. What happens to the water? Does it absorb into one type of soil faster than the other?

6. Construct a small structure using clay and toothpicks. Place the structure on top of the frozen soil. Use toothpicks to secure it in place.

7. Allow the frozen soil to thaw throughout the day. Make note of changes periodically.

8. What happened to the soil as it thawed? How did it affect your structure? How do you think thawing permafrost might affect plant and animal life in the North?

# Further Research

Many books and websites provide information on the environment of Canada's Arctic. To learn more about the environment, borrow books from the library, or surf the Internet.

Most libraries have computers that connect to a database for researching information. If you input a key word, you will be provided with a list of books in the library that contain information on that topic. Nonfiction books are arranged numerically, using their call number. Fiction books are organized alphabetically by the author's last name.

# Books

Banting, Erinn. *Tundras* (Biomes series). New York: Weigl Publishers Inc, 2006.

De Medeiros, Michael. *The North* (Canadian Geographic Regions series). Calgary: Weigl Educational Publishers Limited, 2006.

Tait, Leia and Heather Kissock. *Plants and Animals of the North* (Exploring Canada's Arctic series). Calgary: Weigl Educational Publishers Limited, 2010.

# Websites

To find out more about the Arctic environment and what can be done to help, visit
**http://www.panda.org/what_we_do/where_we_work/arctic/area**.

To learn more about climate change and global warming, visit
**http://epa.gov/climatechange/kids/index.html**.

# Glossary

**acid rain:** air pollution produced when acid chemicals are incorporated into rain, snow, fog, or mist

**ecosystem:** a community of living things sharing an environment

**erosion:** the process of land being worn away by wind, water, or ice

**fossilized:** the process of being turned into stone

**glaciers:** huge masses of ice slowly flowing over a landmass

**greenhouse gases:** atmospheric gases that can reflect heat back to Earth

**seasonal ice:** ice that appears in the colder winter months. It is thinner than glacial ice and does not last as long. Most of it melts in the spring and summer months.

**weathering:** the effects of air, water, or frost on rocks

# Index